RavenWriter

ken goudsward

© 2019 Ken Goudsward
Dimensionfold Publishing
dimensionfold.com

Cover art by Ann Hetmanchuk
www.deviantart.com/alaiaorax

imagination
symbolism
myth

narrative and
 poetry are valid   forms of thought
as valid as analysis
if not more so
deeper

mythic
nonsensical
epic
necessary

Again he sat in the forest. He lay back upon the spongy moss. He stared up with the parallel trunks of trees, reaching toward heaven.

How can light be torn?
There are 5 ways

1 the torn path
2 the torn stream
3 the torn spectrum
4 the torn particle
5 the torn duality

Again he sat on the shore. Waves pounded relentlessly against the rocks. The rocks don't stand a chance.

Three solutions of the classic Cornel tile set will be examined.

A) A simple unconstrained tabletop sliding process is used to attempt proper arrangement/alignment. Upon explosion, tiles are shattered into shards of moderate size on first iteration. Alignment becomes greatly obstructed by non-geometric shard shape. Successive iterations exponentially approach impossibility.

Again he sat in the pond. His eyes at water level. The water licked his eyeballs. It looked strange. He had not yet learned to breathe water, so he did not breathe.

(body)

i want to take my clothes off
i want to be with you naked
and enter you

i want to feel the pleasure of you
the pleasure that is you
the you that is pleasure
i want to turn you into pure pleasure
your pleasure
and mine

but really why do i even care
does it matter
is it really that great
it is fleeting
the wanting is greater than the having
it hypes itself
and i now hardly believe it

i want to take my clothes off
and stretch
and pose
and move
like a tai chi warrior
a mystic yogi
i want to dance like a beach goddess in fire

but i do not dance

Again he sat in the desert. The heat was a physical presence, tangibly washing over him with oppressive pressure. His skin burned. His breath grew dry.

The torn path removes the light from its destiny. It is deflected, reflected, redirected.

how white holes work

one

Again he sat in the forest. He imagined past eons. This place was a glacier, a lake bed, a desert. Right now it is a forest. He is a tree.

Again he sat upon the mountain. His body created an impression in the deep snow. His footprints blew away and were filled in.

Raven	vs	Crow
in the wilderness		in the city
watches life - is life		watches art imitate life
paints with soft brushes		draws
in thick oils on canvas lines		in pen on paper with straight
using textured sweeping spinning strokes		then scans, manipulates, fills renders, prints, publishes
sways in the crown of the tallest spruce		perches on the ledge of an aluminum faceted roof overlooking the city

Again he sat beside the river. The squirrel descended first one tree, then the next. The crows barked incessantly. He tried to decide if the bark of the aspen was green or orange.

(mind)

i want to take my chains off
i want to step out from this little box
i want to fly free like a bird
or a spark
ever upward
i want to ascend
to become
something greater
better
bigger
more advanced
more evolved
into a higher state

but does such a state exist
or is it just another phenomenal artefact
illusory principle

i want to connect with you
we do but
is it enough
we want to connect with that higher being
is he/she enough
is this real

Again he sat beside the river. The cottonwoods bare. Their broken tops scratching the blue clear spring sky. The river was invisible. Still beneath a scab of white. But not still. Waters run beneath. A brown mallard, and one green-headed, winging westward, still seeking open water. A downy feather drifts to earth and lands on dirty ice.

The torn spectrum disrupts the breadth of light. It is narrowed, named, defined, analyzed, dis-integrated, and removed from community.

Again he sat beside the river. Giant ancient beasts lurked in its hidden depths - its deepest pools. Ageless nameless ones with long memory and quick wit. What wisdom persevered only in their collective unconscious?

the beak ^ the claws #
the deep well of eye @
now a spot of growing luminescence
a bright blue void
a chord resounding with
perfect harmonious overtone

the one__both sides
the triple sing-singu-singularity
the five actions
eight words
spill from one sound

echos bounce off charge,
colour, flavour, spin
spun, span, expand
this defines t i m e
PURPOSE
beauty

Again he sat in the forest. Upon a high branch in an old fir. The branch swayed in the strong wind. Its needles occasionally whipped his face.

(end)

will there be an end
of course
will it come soon enough
will it be enough
what is it
must i wait

i want to know
as i am known
if i am known
and if not
what is left

Again he sat upon the mountain. The bear ambled past, uncaring. The cubs followed, but their curiosity caused them to snuff toward him. She did not care. He was not honey.

B) A simple pickup and discard process is employed, with the addition of a discard box of adequate size to accommodate generational growth. Explosion is redefined as puffing into third dimension with semi-randomized geometries. Generational iteration tends toward natural irregular space filling algorithms, rather than successive vertical expansion. Speed of pickup becomes limiting factor during successive iterations.

                                    /
                    two is a divider
                   positive/negative
                       yet attractive
                   i charge toward you
                  you become a magnet
                  even this is a division
                          a dimension
          our planarity enables vectors
        so then, is this space   (point.)
                     here too are waves
                             thus, time
                   and there was light

Again he sat beside the river. The sunshine warmed his face. This year, the snow was not so much melting as dissolving into the sky.

(spirit)

i feel
barely
yet
that i am eternal
that i do transcend
that i am
and you are
and somehow that matters

that we connect
that we are intertwined
that we are together

that somehow time is defined by our together-ness
and that after that and before that is a different type
outside of time
more together more complete
beyond

Again he sat upon the mountain. The rain streamed down like a skyborn river for three days and nights. It felt not at all like sitting in the pond.

birds
when captured <may>
exhibit unconventional facial
features : shapes
their captivity
arouses non standardized
colourations
nuances of plumage
little wonder <some>
prefer their solitude
in the wild

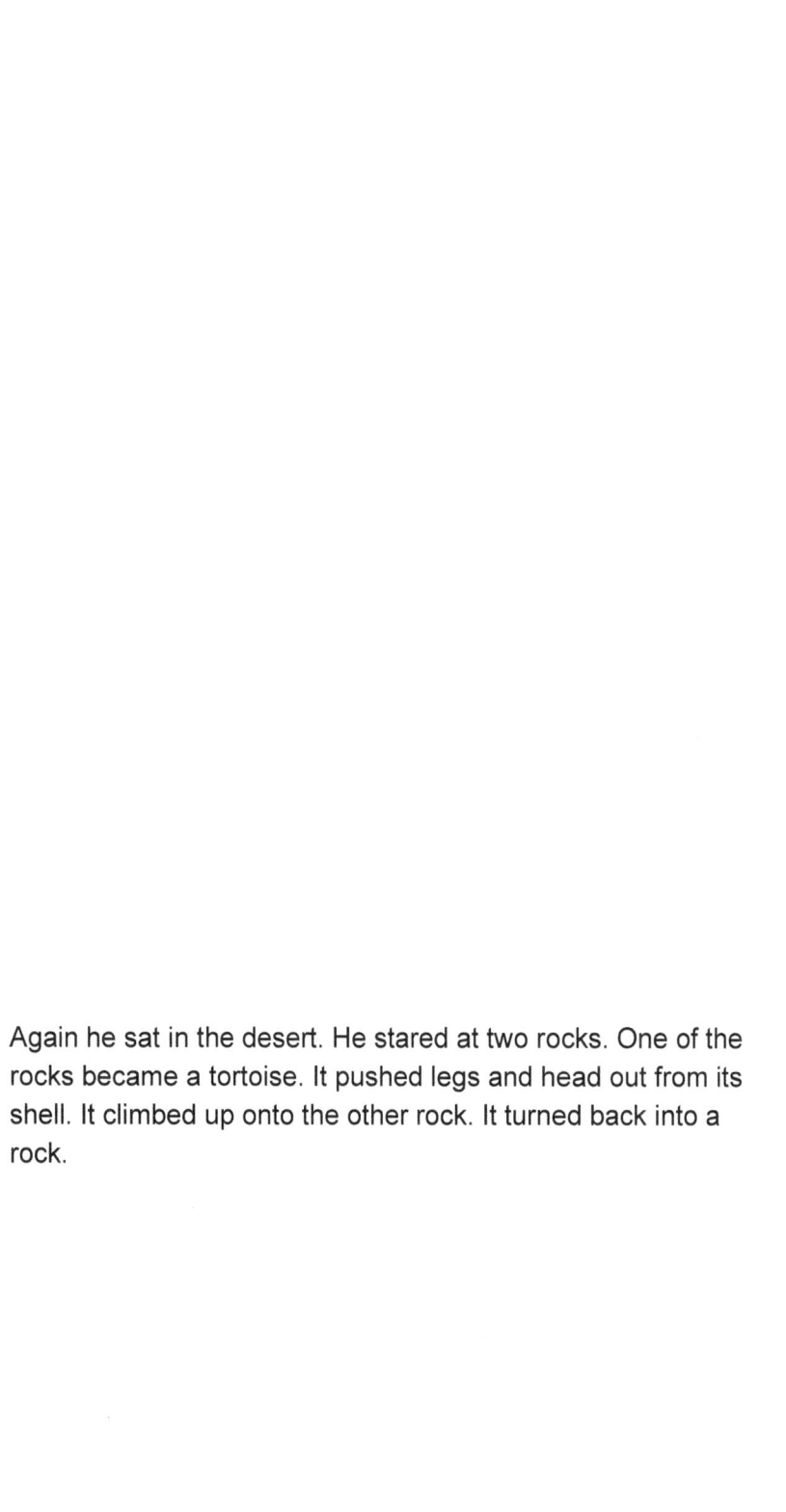

Again he sat in the desert. He stared at two rocks. One of the rocks became a tortoise. It pushed legs and head out from its shell. It climbed up onto the other rock. It turned back into a rock.

(sex)

and then
because
we are connected
because
we are eternal
because
we are transcendent
somehow it all matters

that we connect
that we are intertwined
that we are together

that somehow time is defined by our together-ness
and we create time by our union
and we define space by our touching
by our connecting and overlapping and enveloping
by our naked definition
we define all
by our pleasure
we define pleasure
and by hiding nothing
we define truth

The torn stream interrupts the continuity of the light.
It is fragmented, digitized, packetized, bite-sized.

Again he sat in the desert. There were only rocks. The sand was only smaller rocks. The mountain was only bigger rocks. He became a rock.

He who sat asked the Tyger, "Are stars and people the same?"
"Stars are stars, people are people."
"Well, are they connected"
"Of course"
"How?"
"What do you mean, how?"
"Well, what kind of connection is it?"
"The kind that connect people and stars."

a starry centrifuge
cords [chords] tied at a point
a feather - blacker than black
a diamond
a book /
a brick /   a slow furnace
a magnetic transducer
each reacting to each other's pull

Again he sat in the desert. Nothing moved. Later, a small beetle appeared. It went about its business. Later, a small bird landed. It watched he who sat. It watched the beetle. It ate the beetle. It went about its business.

Again he sat upon the mountain. He saw that the mountain was not real. It was only the negative space between the valleys. It was only what yet remained as the rivers carved it away.

(heart)

i hear this hard truth
small and fleeing bits of joy
may be all we get
an occasional glimpse
of a long soaring view
a cedar tree at 100 kph
a river a star
a rock
perhaps now and then we may
cross an intersection diagonally
the wind in our hair
but never wearing our favorite t-shirt

The torn particle represses the individuality of light. It is homogenized, prepackaged, sterilized, and molded into a line.

◿
three
steps into the space
wraps the two
defines size
adds two more
+/-
becoming three and also four
proposing perspective
scalar ambiguity
strong/weak
strong + weak
provides a pivot
a core
an identity
the ten thousand things
and an anchor

Again he sat upon the mountain. The gnats bit at him. He remained open. The gnats drank his blood. They carried away his blood to the far reaches of the forest, down the mountain, across the valley. They carried his blood. His blood covered the forest. He was everywhere.

It was a cold january day
A raven was there, in the midst
Of a murder
      Of crows
We rattled our beaks at each other
He and I
He did not mind hanging
Out with those crows

Again he sat upon the mountain. The scents of pollen, nectar, and sap drifted and swirled slowly, almost visibly. He tasted them, gaining nourishment.

shapes carved
in ebony
values fill this textiled matrix
threads evolve tiled texts
mated bits
baited mixes
solve salved valves
slaved sliders save max fate
fame flakes peel in helical reels
skull hinge swings
lid locks
click, fall open, counterweighted
tendon tau[gh]t
joint pursed
corpuscle loaded

Again he sat in the pond. His upper lip at water level. He slightly sipped the pond. He could have drank the entire pond; but then there would be no pond to sit in.

The torn duality leverages a decision from light. It is tricked into a false dichotomy, brainwashed, guilt-tripped, henpecked, and forced to choose sides.

(us)

us is the only real joy
mundane perhaps
cliche for sure
but you could not be any better
were you made of cedar
and rock
and wind
for you are all those
and a river and a star
and a long journey
and a warm hearth
and a full flagon

Again he sat on the shore. Sand alternated wet and dry, lapped by gentle waves and breezes.

a leaf falls silently
rotates through a half turn
against a blank sky
a white fingerprint
on a dark wall
a labyrinth of worn stone
snaps suddenly from the left side

Again he sat upon the mountain. The rocks were once deep inside the earth.

C) Initial iterations may be disregarded. Sharding occurs as in solution (A). Several iterations are suggested in order to obtain sufficient fracturing to ensure adequate shard caliber similitude. Remnants can now be swept up with a dry cloth and discarded.

Again he sat on the shore. A bird took off from a rock. It flew in circles. It dove into the water. The bird and the fish emerged, and both flew into the distance.

*

three and four unfold
creating another (generality)
enveloping all (specifics)
the identicals
and the differents
now all together
or eventually
and indistinguishable from a certain point
rolling all back into one

Again he sat in the pond. His chin at water level. The pond became his beard, stretching out grey green into the forest, many tiny incoming streams reaching out like impossibly long fingers, bringing back nutrients, information. He began to sense the change in season. He began to breathe the forest itself. It smells like cool mud on a hot stone.

Again he sat upon the sky. Each previous seat had been glorious in their own way. The sky was glorious in a different way.

www.ingramcontent.com/pod-product-compliance
Lightning Source LLC
Chambersburg PA
CBHW060413080526
44583CB00012B/552